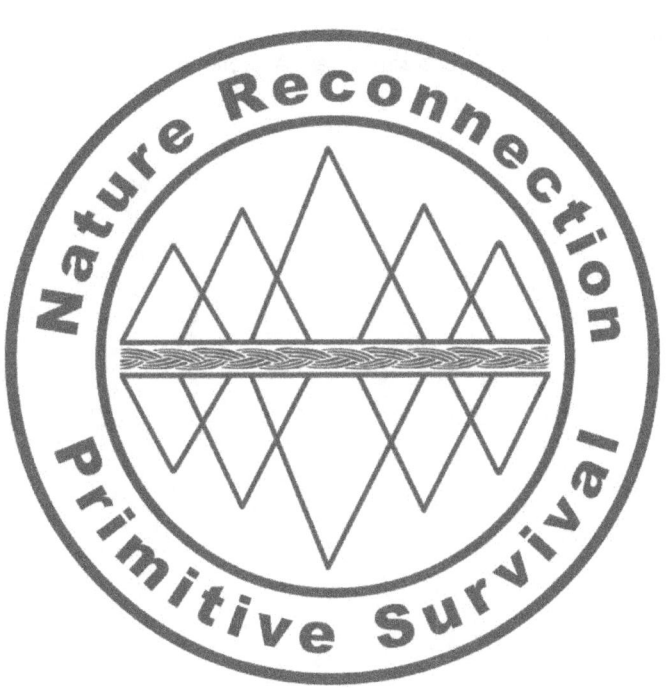

Written by Chad Keel
Illustrations by Kody Sherwood

This book is dedicated to my unborn child, Coyote and
soon-to-be mother, Angelica.

Introduction

Hello, and thank you for buying my book on how to master the art of friction fire. Before outlining everything you need to know, I wanted to take the time to tell you a little about myself. If you simply want the information on how to master the art of friction fire with no stories attached simply flip to chapter one and start.

I think it's important to tell my story, so that you can get an insight into my experience and what type of determination I have put into wholeheartedly learning this craft. Although the title says "mastering the art of friction fire" I need to express that I do not view myself as a master. I am someone with a lot of experience that has had the opportunity to train with top instructors around the world, that being said, I am forever a student. The experience and knowledge I have gained I complied in this book to make your process a fun experience that hopefully leads you deeper into your quest to reconnect with nature.

I took an interest in connecting to the wilderness at a young age mostly because of my dad's influence. He was an outdoorsman and being a man of little means we spent most of our time together in the wilderness areas of Southern California and Western Arizona. I was a wild child building primitive shelters and tree houses, while frog and snake hunting for fun. At this point I didn't think I was learning skills that I would go on to teach to others, I was simply having fun with my dad and brothers.

Around the age of 20 I moved to Hawaii with my brother with the intention of finding a new meaning within ourselves. Hawaii's natural beauty spoke deeply to me and put me on a deeper quest to connect with nature. I began to work with Hawaii's eco-tourism association, having experience with web design and event planning. From there we worked on agricultural restoration of ancient heiau's and I knew I was on the right path working that close to nature.

While working at a heiau dedicated to the Hawaiian God Loki, I began to chat with an elder about Hawaii's rich history.

I had learned a lot and had a lot to share, she was impressed, but told me something powerful "you will one day have to learn about the land where you were born".
This hit me hard. Why did I have to leave my home to find myself and be closer to nature, when nature was all around us? I was depressed, anxious and running from my problems; nature really did heal me. I didn't have to go to Hawaii to figure that out. All nature has the ability to heal us and what better place than in our own backyards. I wanted everyone to have a deeper connection with the earth, and I began to hash out an idea that eventually led me to the place I sit today, writing this book.

Nature Reconnection, a powerful set of words. It insinuates that you already have the connection but lost it somewhere along the way. We reconnect because our ancestors did just that for thousands of years, and the information is still within us, waiting to be awoken once again. So, with these two words I moved back to California with the idea of wholeheartedly reconnecting with the wilderness regions of my homeland.

Hawaii had a rich history and the people knew the story of their ancestors, so how could I reconnect with mine? In my mind, primitive skills felt like the correct path. I spent so much time in nature building shelters, hunting, and camping but didn't have a lot of knowledge of friction fire or other primitive living skills. In my quest I sought out primitive survival instructors and took courses, workshops, and spent long hours practicing. This went on for years.

When I first successfully made friction fire I was hooked. I spent hours and hours practicing, which to this day I continue to do. Coming from a martial arts background I understand that to truly master something you need to apply yourself and spend long hours practicing to polish any skill. I also believe in testing the skill in practical ways that demonstrate your ability to perform in any circumstance.

I instantly became engulfed in the full lifestyle and dedicated myself to learning every skill I possibly could. My brothers and I were going out to build primitive shelters, spending nights on end living primitively in the mountains of California.

By 2014 I had a full realization of what I wanted to do with my pursuit to reconnect with nature. I began hosting "nature reconnection" events in local wilderness areas around where I was living. These events were mostly hiking, and meditation based with me demonstrating some basic primitive skills. Research shows that spending time in nature can aid in improving physical and mental health, and I felt primitive skills were the perfect medicine.

Starting from a place in my heart the events grew fast and the primitive skills became more popular amongst the people attending. My instagram account started to grow and word was spreading that there was a guy teaching people meditation and primitive skills in the wilderness. A few years after starting my classes talent scouts asked me to teach survival on a TV show on the Oxygen Network. My brother and I filmed that episode and shortly after I was approached by talent scouts working for the Discovery Channel. I filmed a survival episode for them on an active volcanic island in the West Indies called Monserrat. In a wet forest after continuous rainfall I was able to make friction fire with a bow drill.

After coming back from Montserrat things began to move very fast. I was now traveling around the world and learning from survival experts in different terrains and environments. In Costa Rica I was made an honorary survival instructor for the Amazonas Survival School after training and sharing knowledge in the jungle and mountain cloud forests. Soon after I filmed another survival show (yet to be disclosed) where I again made friction fire in an extreme survival situation. In the Northern areas of Pakistan, I taught friction fire workshops at high elevations discovering new insights in preparation and technique. In Africa I learned hand drill techniques from bushmen and got a live look into friction fire's primitive roots.

I tell you all this not to brag, but to give you a peek into my background in nature and friction fire. I will forever be a student of friction fire, we can always improve, but this book can serve as a template anyone can grow from.

Preface

This short manual was written to be a reference in the field for anyone interested in the art of friction fire. I outlined two friction fire methods, materials, characteristics, how-to build the working parts, preparation, tinder-building, and finally techniques learned from instructors around the world. To make this manual easy to use in the field I outlined each friction fire method in a single chapter. I recommend getting proficient at each method and remaining a student of nature. Nature is the greatest teacher when it comes to understanding friction fire.

Our ancestors have been doing this for over 300,000 years. The art of mastering and controlling fire was a major factor in humanities success on this planet. Reconnecting with this primitive skill is a feeling that no-one could ever describe to you, you simply need to experience it.

All this being said, lighting any fire without the proper permits in a wilderness area is completely irresponsible. With wild fires becoming so rampant this author was hesitant to even write this book. Giving the reader this knowledge without the experience from an instructor where fire safety is intertwined seemed reckless. This book should serve as a testimony to the deep respect, knowledge and understanding you must have to create friction fires with your bare hands. A student of friction fire is a student of fire safety and there is no separation. Learning to create a fire with your hands will give you the deepest respect for nature, and all her possibilities. Let's get started.

Chapter 1

Preparation

Kindling and Tinder Building

Preparation is the key ingredient for a successful friction fire. You should never attempt to start a fire without the proper preparation for success. There is nothing more disheartening then achieving an ember and not having the proper tinder to ignite the ember into a flame. Starting a fire without enough kindling could cause the flame to die due to not having enough small kindling to feed the flame during its precious first few minutes of life. Everything must be prepared and in place before you start the drilling. Preparation has to be at least 60% of the effort if not more, and you really can never do enough. Here are the essentials you will need before attempting to make a fire.

Tinder Bundle

The tinder bundle is a crucial part of converting the ember made with your friction fire set into a fully ignited flame. The tinder bundle will act as a womb for your ember to nest inside of and grow into a fully developed fire. You will need to take precious time to construct your tinder bundle out of the right materials your ember needs to grow into a flame. While you can create a flame using a single material, such as dried grass, you will have a higher percentage combining materials in a way to help the ember grow. Organize your tinder bundle into a triple layered conglomerate of materials for better success, and a deeper understanding of what your ember needs to grow without resistance.

Fine fibers Group 1

This group will be your tinder bundle's heart, directly in the middle, where you will place your ember. You will need to find or create the finest grain materials so that your ember can burn into them with no resistance or struggle. This group's job is to expand the ember into a large hot spot in the center of the bundle. The finest materials you can find in nature for friction fire will always be thin, fibrous, and dry. Shredded fibers from bark, fibers from palm, shredded dried grass, foam like centers on annual plants, or ground pieces of dried non-poisonous fungi are all examples of this layer.

Sometimes you will need to create this layer and it can be done as an alternative on the fly. You can create multiple feather sticks and collect the shavings. After stock piling a large amount of shaving pulverize the pile on a flat surface into a chunky dust consistency. Regardless of what you use or create the philosophy is this: the ember started in a punk pile of super fine dust and is currently burning contently. First offer it a similar dust pile at the center of your tinder bundle to grow into. Why take the risk of attempting to make an ember ignite larger materials without first letting it grow comfortably?

Medium Fibers Group 2

While the fine fibers group is the hardest to scavenge in nature the medium group should be more readily available. Here you can use dried grass, fibrous coconut husks, thin dried bark, dried animal dung, narrow annual sticks, or anything else that fits these characteristics. The possibilities are always circumstantial to your given environment. The key is to scavenge the driest materials for these groups because a tiny hand drilled ember will most likely not have the heat to overpower damp materials. This is your second largest layer so make sure you scavenge more then you need, just in case you need to add to your tinder bundle as it consumes its fuel.

Largest Fibers Group 3

This will be the bottom layer of your nest and will be the last fibers the ember will make contact with. Here you can use dried bark or grass mixed with small twigs. The plan is to insert your ember into the center of your tinder bundle on top of the fine fibers group. The ember should expand into that group easily and grow relatively fast. As it grows, it will begin to consume the medium fibers below the finest fiber group. This large hot spot will increase the embers heat immensely. Adding additional oxygen with your breath will push the ember to expand into the larger fiber group and ignite into a flame. Make sure to collect a lot of materials for this group because it can always be used as emergency kindling incase the fire starts to dwindle.

This group also serves as the structure of the tinder bundle and supports all the finer fiber groups. Form this group like a bird's nest around the other fibers for optimal success. After your ember ignites into a flame within the tinder bundle it will still have fuel to burn from this layer.

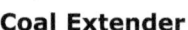

Coal Extender

A coal extender is a material found in nature that can extend the life of your ember and expand its heat into your tinder bundle. If your ember repetitively dies when it is placed inside of your tinder bundle (assuming you are using the correct materials) you may want to try a coal extender to maximize your embers heat and ability to grow into your materials. Good examples are dried fungus, yucca, punk wood, or any material you can find that will easily smolder when touched by an ember. You can use a coal extender in a couple different ways, so give each a try. When you successfully create a friction fire ember take your coal extender and touch it against your ember gently to turn your coal extender into a second ember.

Once they are both smoldering transfer them both into your tinder bundle's center. This will give you two embers, more heat, and a much higher success rate. Another way to use a coal extender, when you create a friction fire ember is to touch your coal extender to your ember gently. Once the ember has transferred into the coal extender and is smoldering on its own place it to the side on top of a small pile of fine fibers group (explained above). This will give you security being that if your original ember does not ignite the tinder bundle on its own you can quickly add the backup coal extender and pile of fine fibers (group 1) and try again. You can even do a hybrid combination of both these examples giving yourself two embers in the tinder bundle and once backup coal extender standing by in a pile of fine fibers (group 1). Being overly prepared is better than having to restart a friction fire method and produce another ember in a survival situation.

Kindling

Your kindling must be made up of dry wood. If you are in a wet environment you may need to baton wood only using the dry inner core of each piece. The damp pieces can be used later once the fire becomes stable with a large coal base. Finding wood with a dry inner core can be tough in some terrains. In these cases, you will need to scout for dead, freestanding pieces of wood to baton. In wet terrain, pieces of wood lying on the ground are not your best option. Dead branches still connected

---

13

to trees up off the ground are the safest bet. Split and separate your collected wood into 3 groups:

Small Group 1

This group can consist of feather sticks, and thin narrow pieces of dry wood. This group can also include extra tinder left over from your tinder bundle. This group is used in the first few minutes of your fire's life to keep it fueled and strong. If your fire's life starts to dwindle, you will need to add more kindling from this group to increase its intensity, to ignite larger groups of kindling. Take your time to select dry pieces of material, and make sure it's fibrous enough to absorb the flame without resistance. Make sure to have three times what you think you will need. We suggest stocking up one large pile about the size of a basketball before starting a fire.

Medium Group 2

This group is similar to the small kindling group, but the strips of wood are slightly thicker and wider. Because this group is made of larger pieces of wood it will require more heat to ignite it. The heat required to ignite the medium kindling will always come from properly stoking the ember within the smaller kindling group first. This medium pile can be made of small twigs, bark, or baton thin pieces of dry wood. Make sure to have three times what you think you will need. We suggest stocking up two large piles about the size of a basketball before starting a fire.

Large Group 3

This group is not the final wood you aim to burn once the fire is stable, it is a slightly larger group of kindling. The plan is to start the fire inside of your tinder bundle and begin to feed it from the smallest group of kindling. While the burning persists, you should attempt to add pieces from the medium pile. If you notice they are taking flame, you can begin to add more from the medium pile. By this time, you will have a fire but no coal base at the bottom of your flame.

This is where your slightly larger kindling will play out its role in assisting you with larger pieces of wood that will smolder red hot at the base of your flame. Keep feeding it from the medium pile while attempting to add larger kindling into the flame. Once the medium pieces are taking flame and staying lit you can add larger pieces until you build a nice hot coal base at the bottom of your fire. Make sure to have three times what you think you will need. We suggest stocking up two-three large piles each the size of a basketball before starting a fire.

Chapter 2

Hand Drill Friction Fire Method

What you are looking for
Spindle

When looking for a spindle in nature it is essential that you keep your mind open to multiple options. It is hard to find a straight stick at the perfect width and length. Sometimes you will have to create a spindle by shaving down a larger imperfect stick as long as it has the right characteristics.

Hardness: Our spindle shouldn't be too hard, as we need it to grind into our hearth board and create dust called punk. Check the wood with your finger nail. Can you scratch the surface with your fingernail and leave an impression? This is a quick way to check the hardness of the wood. That being said, the wood needs to be hard enough not to break from the force required to start a friction fire.

Fibers: It is always a good sign to have the fibers running down the length of the spindle. This will give the spindle strength, and helps the fiber break down as its ground into the hearth board while reducing polishing. If you are shaving a spindle down from a larger imperfect stick, make sure your fibers are running down the length of the spindle opposed to running the width.

Hearth Board

Hearth boards are much easier to find, but the characteristics are just as important.

You will need to split and baton wood to create a hearth board, or find a stick larger than your spindle, flatten it out, and add your notch. When selecting materials for a hearth board you need to compliment your spindles hardness. It is wise to have a hearth board that is a little harder than
your spindle. If your spindle is made of a harder wood it will most likely drill through your hearth board before you create an ember. All smoke and no flame. With a slightly softer spindle, the hearth board resists the spindle just enough to allow grinding which produces ample punk(dust).

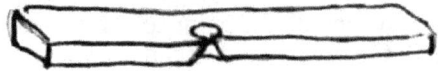

Working the parts:
Spindle

A hand drill should be about the size of your pinky finger. If your stick is wider in width, you will need to shave it down carefully until it is at the correct circumference. For length, "The longer the Better", but it is very hard to find a long straight stick with the strength to withstand the hand drill method. Over eleven Inches in length is more than enough for a beginner. Smooth your spindle after you have completed its final shape. You can rub the spindle against different grains of rocks until it feels comfortable inbetween your hands with no painful areas. You can add small amounts of tree sap to your spindle for extra traction.

Hearth Board

Your hearth board should be about 1/2 of an inch in thickness. Making it thicker will only require additional work 'regarding the punk build up' required to reach the heat of the spindle and ignite the piles pinnacle.

Regarding length, it is really preference. For beginning students of the hand drill, it is wise to have a longer hearth board to hold with your feet or with rocks while drilling. The width of the top platform is another preference. Do you want to do two rows of holes? These are preferences.

Pre-drilling

Place your spindle on your heath boards platform a quarter inch back from the drilling edge. Remove the spindle and mark an indent on the hearth board roughly around center, where the spindle was. Take a rock or knife and make a crude depression on the hearth boards platform for your spindle to balance. After, referring to "techniques", start your hand drilling until you make your spindle and hearth board smoke. This will blacken your depression and show you where to cut your notch properly.

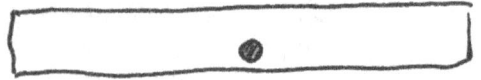

Cutting the Notch

After pre-drilling, you can cut your notch aiming near center of the burn hole. The plan is to cut a pie shape with its tip aimed at, or near the burn hole's center. The tip should come just short of the center of the burn hole. Take your cutting instrument and place it on the platform of your hearth board. Press down and score the hearth board where you will make your cuts. On the drilling edge, you can slope away from the center slightly. After scoring your template with your cutting instrument, carefully begging removing the wood forming your notch. Be careful not to pass the burn hole's center, and never make the notch wider than the spindle. If you do, the spindle will fall out of the burn hole and destroy your punk pile. If the notch is to narrow it will clog up the notch and not allow the punk to build up uniformly inside of the notch. If you are getting a lot of smoke, remember the punk needs to build up from the tray underneath the hearth board until it touches the bottom of the spindle.

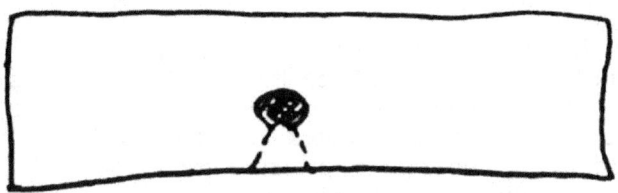

Ember Tray

The ember tray is a flat material placed underneath the hearth boards notch to catch the punk and ember, so it can be transported to the tinder bundle after ignition. You can use any flat thin surface like bark, a flat rock, or even a leaf. Place it underneath your hearth boards drilling edge. Position it directly under your notch with about an inch over hang. This tray will help collect and transport your ember in the important moments of friction fire.

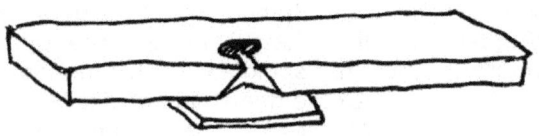

Techniques

These are the techniques used for the hand drill, and should be practiced consistently to condition the hands, and understand how to breathe. There are two types of pressure needed to create a friction fire using the hand drill. Pressure needs to be placed into the spindle to keep it stable while the drilling technique is being performed. Pressure also needs to be placed down into to hearth board simultaneously while drilling.

So, while applying pressure into the spindle we are also applying heavy weighted pressure down into the hearth board.

All this pressure and friction can quickly take its toll on your hands, and you will feel it deep into your bones. Do not burn and blister your hands in one sitting, be patient. Set aside 10 minutes a day for your friction fire workout, practice putting pressure into your spindle while grinding the spindle into your hearth board.

If you are polishing your hearth boards hole and not creating lots of dust you need to work on creating more downward pressure. Any time you feel any blistering coming about, put your kit down for a couple days and then restart again. Eventually you will have the conditioning to create a friction fire without damaging your hands.

Traveling

This is the first and easiest technique to start with while learning the hand drill. You start by placing the spindle into your burn hole and placing your hands at the top of the spindle. Pull one hand back towards you while you push the other hand forward. Keep the spindle balanced in rotation between your hands.

Use the entire length of your hands, and don't get into the habit of making small strokes. Starting at the top you work your way down the spindle with this motion putting pressure down into the hearth board. Each time you reach the bottom you restart at the top and repeat the process.

Always using the length of your hands, you can isolate the top, middle, and bottom lanes of your hand, and use those lanes separately to increase performance. Once you are traveling consistently and keeping the spindle inside of the hole, you only need persistence. Assuming your hands are conditioned (like I recommended) you will need to continue traveling until your punk pile ignites into an ember.

Just because you have made smoke does not mean you are close to creating an ember. Remember, the punk pile needs to build up high enough to touch the spindle's bottom to ignite. So, if you are smoking but your pile of punk is still low, do not burn yourself out. Stay consistent and build that punk pile to a proper height and you will have success.

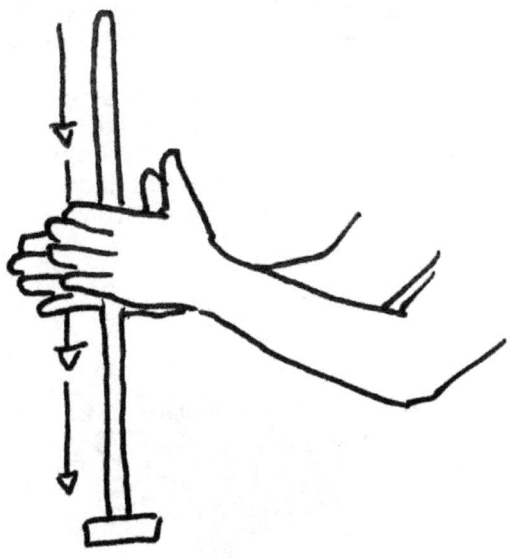

Floating

Floating is a technique where your hands do not travel to the bottom of the spindle during motion but remain at the top of the spindle. This is done by a circular motion being created with the hands while stroking back and forth. Like the traveling technique one hand is pulled back towards the driller, and one hand is pushed forward while keeping the spindle in-between their hands.
The main difference is before the hand going forward reaches its resolution it tilts up aiming its fingers towards the sky.
The hand moving back aims its fingers gently down towards the ground creating a circular motion within the palms of the two hands. The motion spins the spindle while also giving the driller enough friction to press down into the hearth board. Proper technique will allow the drillers hands to remain in place, and with enough practice you will be able to start a friction fire without traveling.
 Floating will allow you to apply continuous motion and not stop to reset like the traveling technique requires. Floating will also allow the driller to use shorter spindles. This is because you do not need a long spindle to 'travel down' to produce the force needed for friction fire.

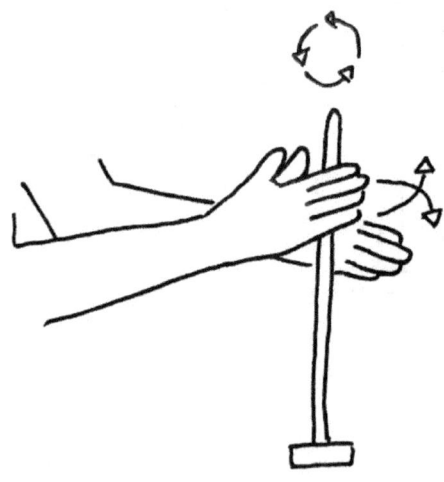

Combo

Combination of these two techniques is super common. Some people might float the entire process until the punk has reached the bottom of the spindle, and will then begin rapidly traveling to produce extra downwards pressure for final ignition. Some will float for a couple seconds and then travel down half of the spindle and float their way back to the top. Floating with light pressure into the mid-spindle can allow your hands to float back to the top of the spindle while in continuous motion. With this understanding, you can float at the top of the spindle, travel down for extra pressure, and float back to the top and repeat this process until ignition. Using a healthy combination will allow you to use a majority of your spindles surface area in continuous motion. One should be proficient at creating an ember from both traveling and floating before experimenting with combos.

Postures and Positioning

There are a lot of different ways to sit or kneel while creating a friction fire, but we will outline the solid, proven techniques. Posture is important with every possible position outlined, so take your time to get comfortable. Use your skeletal system to the best of your advantage and remember to breathe. It's very easy to exhaust yourself while creating a friction fire. Exhaustion is the number one reason people fail while attempting to make an ember. Sit with the upmost attention to your posture so that you can maintain your position throughout the entire process without pain or discomfort.

Sitting Butterfly

The sitting butterfly is a lot like the sitting butterfly stretch commonly taught in most physical education, or sports conditioning.

For this position, you will sit with your hearth board and ember tray directly in front of you. The notch should be facing you and your feet should be placed on each side of the hearth board to keep it firmly on the ground. Use the outer edge of your foot and open your knee's wide similar to the butter fly stretch and relax. This will be your positing through the process of creating an ember. Practice sitting in this position, holding down the hearth board with your feet, and spinning the spindle with your hands. You may need to move your butt forward or backwards to find the perfect sweet spot for maximum RPM's on the spindle.

Sitting Open

This position is similar to the butterfly, but you only put one foot on the hearth board or sit in easy pose in front of your hearth board. If you choose to sit in easy pose you will need to support the hearth board with rocks, or from a partner while you spin the spindle. The notch should be facing you, so you can observe the punk build up along the way. Pay attention to your posture and make adjustments before you start your process. Once in motion you should remain consistent and see the process through until you create an ember.

Kneeling

Kneeling will allow you to have a lot of force down into the hearth board because you can use the weight of your head and torso. Like easy pose you will need to support your hearth board because you will not be holding it with your feet. The notch should be facing you, so you can be aware of when the ember is ignited, or if you need to apply more pressure.
 While pressing into the spindle you can hover your head and torso almost above the spindle allowing your weight to travel down the shaft into the hearth board.

This position will allow you to create the most force naturally because of mechanics and gravity. While you can easily kneel and float your hands, this position favors traveling. This is because you can travel while applying massive amounts of weight with your head and torso above the spindle.

Breathing

With all the moving parts and techniques, it's easy to forget to breathe and quickly exhaust your body during the intense energy release friction fire requires. This is what you need to know. Focus on your breath above flawless technique because even sloppy technique can produce an ember if the driller has consistency and doesn't let up. It is so common to tense up and forget to breathe when we are applying pressure into a piece of wood in motion. If we run out of breath, we will not be able to produce an ember because we will not have the force and consistency required. Find a repetition to your breathing from the very start and maintain it throughout the entire process. Having control over your breathing will allow smooth, and consistent revolutions of the spindle which is optimal for an embers creation. Healthy controlled breathing during this strenuous activity will allow blood to circulate oxygen to your working muscles. As you are focusing on proper form and pressure, it can be easy to forget about your breathing or even hold your breath. As challenging as friction fire is to a beginner improper breathing can make friction fire that much more challenging. take the time to practice proper breathing. This is the secret step towards improving the quality of your technique.

Sitting Butterfly

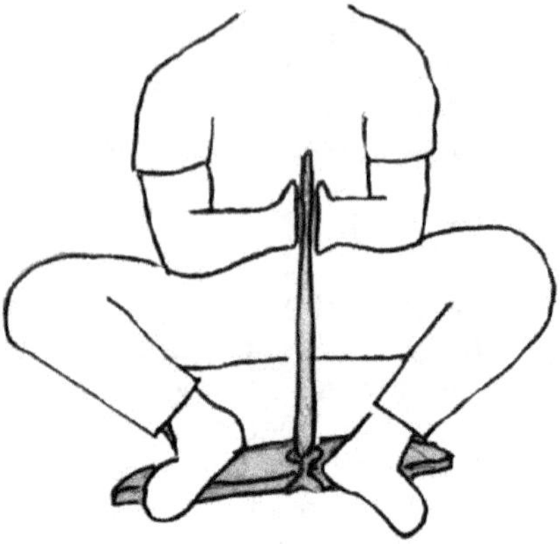

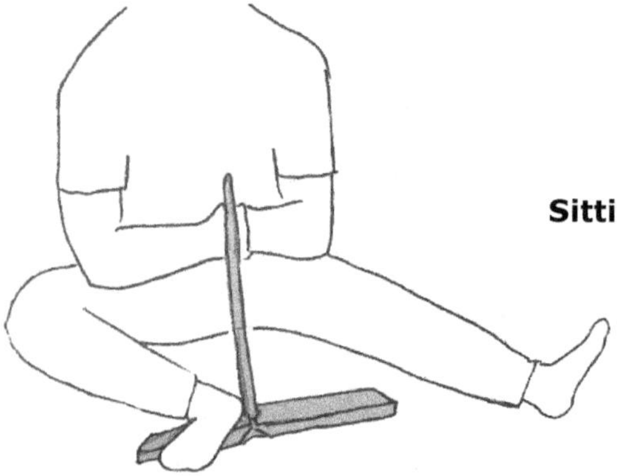

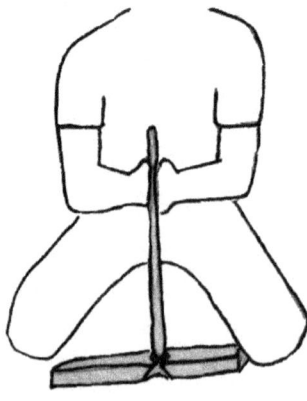

Sitting Open

Kneeling

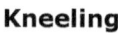

Chapter 3

Bow Drill Friction Fire Method

What you are looking for

Spindle

The spindle for a bow drill is much larger then ones needed for a hand drill. A spindle for a bow drill is about the length between your elbow and wrist, although it can be much smaller. The circumference of the spindle can also vary due to preference. But usually a spindles circumference for a bow drill will be about the size of your thumb and larger. The Key is finding semi-straight sticks in nature suitable for friction fire. Not all sticks are created equal when it comes to friction fire. Sometimes you will find sticks or materials that work perfectly with little crafting needed. Most of the time you will have to create a spindle by shaving down a larger imperfect stick, as long as it has the right characteristics.

Hardness

Our spindle shouldn't be too hard, as we need it to grind into our hearth board and create dust called punk. Check the wood with your finger nail. Can you scratch the surface with your fingernail and leave an impression? This is a quick way to check the hardness of the wood. That being said, the wood needs to be hard enough not to break from the force required to start a friction fire.

Fibers

It is always a good sign to have the fibers running down the length of the spindle. This will give the spindle strength, and helps the fiber break down as its ground into the hearth board while reducing polishing.

If you are shaving a spindle down from a larger imperfect stick, make sure your fibers are running down the length of the spindle opposed to running the width.

Top Block

The top block or bearing block is a piece of your kit held in your hand during the bow drill process. This piece acts as a bearing holding the spindle in place during the drilling process. The top block will also allow the driller to apply pressure down into the hearth board. This piece can be made of virtually anything, but it is important that it fits comfortably in your hand. The bottom of your top block must have an impression to hold the spindle in place while in motion. This impression can be created easily with a rock or knife depending on the hardness of the material you use. Stone, bone, antler and most commonly wood is used for this piece of your bow drill kit. The piece should be a little bigger then the palm of the drillers hand and should fit comfortably. Take time to shape and smooth this piece out, as most of your bodies weight will rest on top of it.

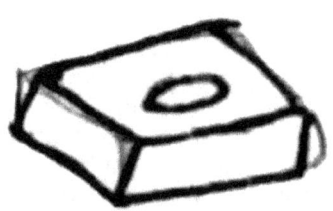

Hearth Board

When selecting materials for a hearth board you need to compliment your spindles hardness. It is wise to have a hearth board that is a little harder than your spindle. If your spindle is made of a harder wood it will most likely drill through your hearth board before you create an ember. All smoke and no flame. With a slightly softer spindle the hearth board resists the spindle just enough to allow grinding which produces ample punk. Hearth boards are much easier to find, but the characteristics are just as important. You will need to split and baton wood to create a hearth board or find a stick larger than your spindle. The length of your hearth board will depend on preference, but a good reference in the length between your elbow and wrist.

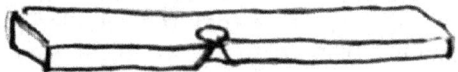

Bow

 The bow of your kit will be the power mechanism of this ancient technology. You will be looking for a strong stick with a natural bow or arch about the length between your wrist and shoulder. The bow can be smaller depending on preference, and some also prefer a near straight stick as opposed to the arched bow. Try both and see which one you prefer based on performance. Smooth your bows handle so that you can hold it easily during the process. Sometimes you will need to notch you bow to hold your cordage without it slipping during the intensity of bow drilling for a friction fire. The bow really should be found in near working condition for survival purposes, but there is nothing wrong with creating something beautiful worth carry around for multiple uses.

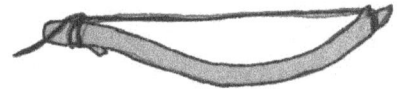

Cordage

Cordage for a bow drill can be made in nature, while a shoelace from your shoe can work much faster. If you plan to take the complete primitive route you will need to identify materials in your environment to create cordage. This is a complete skill set you should already understand completely before attempting to create cordage strong enough to withstand the friction placed upon it during the bow drill process. Assuming you understand the basics of making primitive cordage, and you have identified your material you can use reverse-wrapping to strengthen it. You will need to do doubled or tripled reverse wrapping in most cases to make the cordage strong enough, and this can take some time to complete. Your cordage needs to tie to one end of your bow drill and wrap around the handle end snuggly, so it needs to be longer than your bow. So, plan to make the cordage a half size larger than the total length of your bow. If you are using a show lace or para-cord you should not have any issues although bow drilling can destroy fibers quickly. A typical shoe lace in a survival situation should get you one to three fires before breaking down and breaking. In desperate times, you could cut stands from your clothing and reverse wrap it into a strong cordage capable of withstanding a few valiant goes at a bow drill friction fire. While using shoelaces, and para-cord is easier, it is essential to learn how to identify materials and create cordage in nature on your own.

Working the parts

Spindle

A bow drill should be slightly larger than your thumb when it is finished. If your stick is wider in circumference, you will need to shave it down carefully until it is at the correct circumference. The spindle should be about the length of your wrist to your elbow. The spindle does not need to be that long, but it should be made as straight as possible. Smooth your spindle after you have completed its final shape. You can rub the spindle against different grains of rocks until it feels smooth. Rough areas will only further damage your cordage during the drilling process. Your spindle should be relatively flat on the drilling side. This is because we want it to grind into the hearth board, and not bore a hole. The top of the spindle going into the top black can be rounded to reduce friction.

Top Block

The top block can be made of any material you choose and is used to hold the spindle in place while the drilling is taking place. People use wood, antler, bone, or even rocks for this piece. Just make sure it fits comfortably inside of your hand while applying the downward pressure. Once you decide on your material you should shape it to fit inside the palm of your hand. The bottom should be flattened, and an indent should be added to the center.

The indent must be large enough for the spindle to fit inside and not slide out. Although the friction should happen where the spindle meets the hearth board it is common for the top block to smoke and heat up as well. This is unwanted because we want the spindle to rotate freely within the top block. We want all the friction going into the hearth board. A way to reduce this upper friction is to add green plant matter inside the indent of the top block. The spindle will grind the plant matter into a moist lubrication reducing the friction and allowing the spindle to rotate freely up top.

Hearth Board

 Flatten the bottom of your hearth board so that it sits flat to the ground. Your hearth board should be about 1/2 of an inch to a full inch in width. Any wider will only require additional work regarding the punk build up required to reach the heat of the spindle and ignite the piles pinnacle. Regarding length, it is really preference. For beginning students of the hand drill, it is wise to have a longer hearth board to hold with your feet or with rocks while drilling. The width of the top platform is another preference. Do you want to do two rows of holes? These are preferences.

Bow

The Bow is a crucial component to this ancient method of creating fire. Although it is an important piece to your kit it will be easier to find then the spindle or hearth board. While those two require a certain type of wood the bow itself can be made of virtually any material. If you are sourcing everything from the wilderness you will be looking for a stick about the distance from your wrist to shoulder. The stick should fit comfortably inside of your hand and should be strong enough to take the pressure of bow drilling. Your bow can be straight or have a slight curve. Add a notch to the top of your bow and secure your cordage. Then pull the cordage tight to the bottom of your bow and wrap the cordage around the handle to secure it. Your hand will hold the tension of the bow's string while you drill.

Cordage

Cordage can be natural or artificial when making a bow drill string. If you are attempting this for the first time it is recommended you practice using artificial cordage such as 550 cord (para-cord). Once you develop the skills necessary to create an ember and feel you are ready for a new challenge you can attempt creating cordage. The cordage you use must be strong and durable to take the heat and friction applied from the spindle rotating. If you attempt primitive cordage use a reverse wrap two ply method of your material choice. It is recommended to combine two or three reverse wrapped lengths for extra strength. Remember to make it longer then the length of your bow so that you can secure it to the bow.

Techniques

The basic drilling posture: Here the practitioner has their non-dominate foot forward applying pressure to the hearth board. The dominate leg is behind the body with the knee down on the ground. The spindle is wrapped into the cordage of the bow with the spindle ending up on the outside. It is important for the spindle to be on the outside of the bow. If the spindle ends up between your bow and the cordage rewrap it before starting. Position the wrapped cordage near the bottom or 'base' of the spindle to start. The non-dominate hand will hold the top block and support the spindle. Make sure your non-dominate shoulder is positioned over your non-dominate hand holding the spindle. The dominate hand will hold the bow and complete the strokes that spin the spindle consistently. Using your skeletal system is crucial to success and pressure. You don't want to be shaky or unstable while creating an ember. To create the ember begin stroking the bow back and forth spinning the spindle. Keep consistent pressure for an ember.

Elbow Outside of the knee

While positioning your posture you will need to make a decision on where to place your elbow. The non-dominate elbow will need to be held close to the knee of the non-dominate leg for support. If you place the elbow to the outside of the non-dominate knee you can lock your whole body into a secure posture. The posture must be maintained until the ember is created, so ensure you are comfortable.

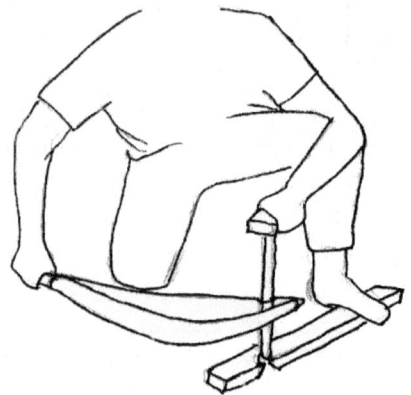

Elbow Inside of the knee

While positioning your posture you will need to make a decision on where to place your elbow. The non-dominate elbow will need to be held close to the knee of the non-dominate leg for support.
If you place the elbow to the inside of the non-dominate knee you can lock your whole body into a secure posture. The elbow will be
supported by the knee and will reduce fatigue and shaking that causes the spindle to slip out of the top block. The posture must be maintained until the ember is created, so ensure you are comfortable.

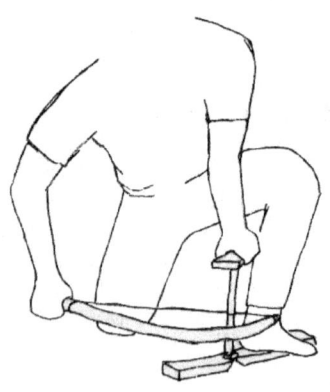

Team Drilling

2 Person: A multiple person bow drill can help to reduce fatigue of an individual by sharing the energy required to start a friction fire. For a two person bow drill you will need to collect all of the materials listed above. The bow is the only piece you will not need. Once all materials are collected and prepared you can begin with creating an ember. One person will sit down with both feet on either side of the hearth board for support. They will use their hands to support the spindle standing upright between the hearth board and top block. Their job is to support the hearth board, and apply the pressure onto the top block while the spindle is rotating. The second person will be on their knees in front of the other person. They will act as "the bow" and make the spindle rotate. Take the cordage and make two loops at each end big enough for two fingers to slip through.

Wrap the cordage around the spindle twice or three times and position yourself on your knees with your fingers through the loops.

Pull the cordage in an outward direction and refrain from pulling straight back towards your body as this will put unnecessary pressure on the spindle. Also notice how the cordage is wrapped around the spindle. One part will be higher on the spindle and one part will be lower. Keep your hands pulling at this same height (one hand pulling higher, and one hand pulling lower) and maintain the wrap as you pull. Keep the spindle rotating consistently until you create an ember.

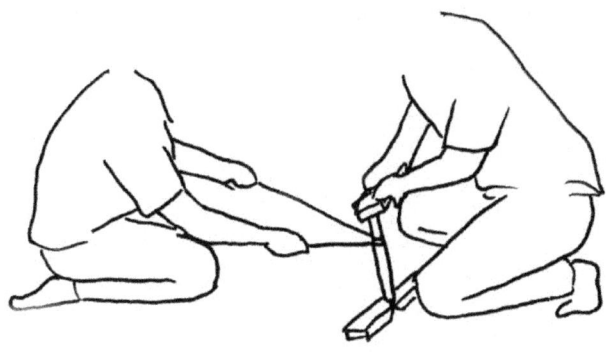

3 Person: A multiple person bow drill can help to reduce fatigue of an individual by sharing the energy required to start a friction fire. For a three person bow drill you will need to collect all of the materials listed above. The bow is the only piece you will not need. Once all materials are collected and prepared you can begin with creating an ember. One person will sit down with both feet on either side of the hearth board for support. They will use their hands to support the spindle standing upright between the hearth board and top block.

Their job is to support the hearth board and apply the pressure onto the top block while the spindle is rotating. The second and third person will be on their knees in front of the hearth board. They will act as "the bow" and make the spindle rotate. Take the cordage and make two loops at each end big enough for two fingers to slip through. Wrap the cordage around the spindle twice or three times and position the two people on their knees with their fingers through the loops.

One person will pull one way, and the other person will pull the opposite way. Pull the cordage in an outward direction and refrain from pulling straight back towards your body as this will put unnecessary pressure on the spindle. Also notice how the cordage is wrapped around the spindle. One part will be higher on the spindle and one part will be lower. Keep your hands pulling at this same height (one hand pulling higher, and one hand pulling lower) and maintain the wrap as you pull. Keep the spindle rotating consistently until you create an ember.

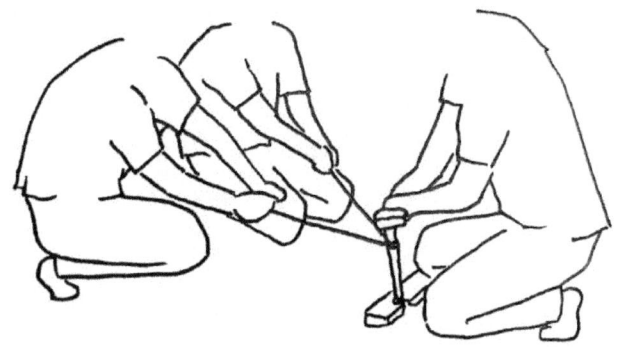

Thank you for reading...

Now you have the essential knowledge to create friction fire. Don't forget to stay consistent with your practice, and don't give up because you didn't get it the first try. Anyone can create friction fire and thusly develop a deeper relationship with nature. Remember to always be responsible about where you practice friction fire. Keeping our forests and wildlands safe is always the main priority.

Tag me on Social Media

I want to see a video of you making a friction fire. Please have my book somewhere in the video and I will share the video on my social media pages. I can't wait to see your success! If you simply want to upload a video review of my book on social media, I would appreciate that as well. Tag me so I can watch your review and share it on my page.